Rosie and Grandad went to school.

'Oh, no!' said Rosie. 'No lunchbox!'

2

Rosie and Grandad went home.

'Oh, no!' said Grandad. 'No key!'

Grandad went into the house.

He got the key.

Rosie and Grandad went to school.

'Oh, no!' said Rosie. 'No lunchbox!'